About This Book

Title: *Working Together*

Step: 6

Word Count: 252

Skills in Focus: All vowel-r combinations

Tricky Words: done, people, community, fall, school, build

Ideas For Using This Book

Before Reading:

- **Comprehension:** Look at the title and cover image together. Walk through the pictures in the book with readers and have them make predictions about what they might learn while reading.
- **Accuracy:** Practice saying the tricky words listed on page 1.
- **Phonics:** Tell students they will read words with the r-controlled vowel combinations *er*, *ir*, *or*, and *ur*. Prepare r-controlled vowel word cards with the words *turn*, *dirt*, *work*, *her*, *bird*, and *hurt*. Have readers identify and underline the vowel-r combination for each word (e.g., the *ur* in *turn*). Read the words together several times. Ask readers, "What is the second sound in each word?" Point out that the sound (/r/) is the same, but it can be spelled *ur*, *ir*, *er*, or *or*. Other times words can be spelled with *ar*, *er*, *ir*, *or*, or *ur*, but we can still hear the vowel sound, as in *sort*. Tell readers that while they read, they will be looking for vowel-r words and listening to how they sound.

During Reading:

- Have readers point under each word as they read it.
- **Decoding:** If readers are stuck on a word, help them say each sound and blend the sounds together smoothly. Point out words with vowel-r combinations as they appear.
- **Comprehension:** Invite readers to talk about new things they are learning about working together while reading. What are they learning that they didn't know before?

After Reading:

Discuss the book. Some ideas for questions:

- What are some ways you work together with others?
- Where do you see people working together in your community?

Working Together

Text by Laura Stickney

Reading Consultant
Deborah MacPhee, PhD
Professor, School of Teaching and Learning
Illinois State University

PICTURE WINDOW BOOKS
a capstone imprint

People work together in many ways.

When people work together, hard work takes less time. The work goes by faster.

People get big jobs done by working together. Each worker does their part.

You can work with others to make your town a better place.

Start a community garden. Grow plants in the dirt.

The garden will turn your town into a nicer place.

People can grow their own food in the garden. They can share the garden.

People can work together to clean up a park.

They can pick up trash like water bottles or wrappers. This work keeps the park clean.

People can work together to help others in their town. They can sort cans of food at a food shelf.

Workers can start to raise cash or gather food for kids in need.

People can work together after a storm. Poor weather may make a big tree fall over in a yard.

The tree may block the road.

People can work together to move the tree out of the yard or road.

They can work to help critters like birds that got hurt in the storm.

Some people work together as part of their jobs.

They work hard to build bridges or barns.

They work hard to fix roads.

You may work with others to do projects at school. You learn to split up the work.

Then you share the project with the class. The class cheers for your hard work!

Working together makes the world a better place!

More Ideas:

Phonics Activity

Play Memory with Vowel-R Combinations:
Prepare two sets of cards (using two different colors) to play a game of Memory. On one set of cards, write vowel-r words from the story. For each word, prepare a separate card of a different color with the corresponding vowel-r spelling. Place the cards face down on a surface. Have students take turns turning two cards over, one of each color. To make a match, the students must read the word on one card and have the correct letter combination on the other. Continue playing until all cards have been matched.

Suggested words:
- *ar*: part, garden, start, park, yard, hard
- *er*: faster, critters, weather, better
- *ir*: dirt, birds
- *or*: work, for, sort, storm, world
- *ur*: turn, hurt

Extended Learning Activity

Make a List:
Ask readers to spend a few minutes thinking about ways they can work together with others. Then have readers write a list of the different ways they can work with others. How does each way of working together help the community? Challenge students to use words with vowel-r combinations in their list.

Published by Picture Window Books, an imprint of Capstone
1710 Roe Crest Drive, North Mankato, Minnesota 56003
capstonepub.com

Copyright © 2026 by Capstone.
All rights reserved. No part of this publication may be reproduced in whole or in part, or stored in a retrieval system, or transmitted in any form or by any means, electronic, mechanical, photocopying, recording, or otherwise, without written permission of the publisher.

Library of Congress Cataloging-in-Publication Data is available on the Library of Congress website.

ISBN: 9798875227271 (hardback)
ISBN: 9798875231483 (paperback)
ISBN: 9798875231469 (eBook PDF)

Image Credits: iStock: FG Trade, 28–29, filmstudio, cover, fotoember, 25, Goodboy Picture Company, 8–9, Memedozaslan, 26–27, RyanJLane, 14, 30–31, 32; Shutterstock: BearFotos, 24, Cherries, 5, DC Studio, 15, Halfpoint, 6–7, Jay Gao, 20–21, Joseph Thomas Photography, 18–19, narikan, 10–11, PeopleImages.com - Yuri A, 22–23, Serhii Bobyk, 4, Stock-Asso, 13, Studio Romantic, 2–3, Ursula Page, 16–17, Zulfiska, 1, 12

Printed and bound in China. 6274